NEW CHATTO POET

NEW CHATTO POETS

ALAN JENKINS

PETER McDONALD

JO SHAPCOTT

DOMINIC FISHER

PIPPA LITTLE

LACHLAN MACKINNON

ADAM THORPE

CHATTO & WINDUS
LONDON

Published in 1986 by
Chatto & Windus Ltd
40 William IV Street
London WC2N 4DF

British Library
Cataloguing in Publication Data
New Chatto poets.
I. Jenkins, Alan
821'.914'08 PR6060.E351/
ISBN 0-7011-3080-6

Phototypeset by Wyvern Typesetting Ltd, Bristol
Printed in Great Britain by
Redwood Burn Ltd
Trowbridge, Wiltshire

CONTENTS

NEW CHATTO POETS

ALAN JENKINS

Party-going

Just finding the place was an act of love.
Signposts, maps deceived us as we drove
And drove, not speaking, through incessant rain.
The windscreen-wipers' rhythmic screech
Ran back and forth, a hot knife
Behind the eyes, entering a nerve or vein.
A stream of water splayed and pumped
Across eye-funnelling black, the downs stepped off
Into nothing, or the few smudged lights that shone
Below; a blurring loom became two headlamps
That bore through us steadily and were gone.
For hours we traced the same roads over fields,
Each track returning with the sense of known shapes
Outside – hedges, trees, massed hills – half-
Defined, the negative of landscapes.

It seemed we might have driven round all night,
And then for ever – locked in a tight
And tightening circle. Miles away,
Tyres bit into gravel, splashed through mud
In cart-tracks leading to the oast-house.
Inside, rooms were fired to a circular blaze,
Painted masks bobbed out of shadow where
Little smoky groups crouched on bare floors.
A pale green face twitched uncontrollably.
Incense and marijuana mixed a pungent air
Thickening round figures you could hardly see,
And the walls had turned the colour of blood
By the time we arrived – or was it

All dreamt up while we were trying to drowse
In a field somewhere, drunk, unfit

To go on? Of morning, all I remember is
The tangled thicket of blackberries
Like smoking entrails, the delicate
Clusters of blood-clots drenched,
And the hedges' crown of thorns
Draped with mist, grey half-light, the quiet;
The long grass under nets of frost;
Then the distant, sudden blare of horns
As if something had been accomplished,
The knowledge coming back that we were lost.
Whatever it was then that I wished,
Some loosening, like a fist unclenched,
Some final warmth – I felt the spreading ache
Through both my arms, and found two holes, two burns
Like those a cigarette might make.

Ties

The dark green Tootal with white spots he wore
in the first photograph of him I saw –
the tie he lent to me for my first date

and later told me I could keep,
the matching scarf too. So 1930s,
I might as well have been in the war.

Two autumn-coloured, large-check ties
that gave me, so I thought, the air
of a schoolmaster out of Evelyn Waugh.

Then the red houndstooth, a bracing affair
with a dash of gin-and-it or *Brighton Rock*,
a lounge-lizard's whiff of the paddock.

The last, that I've worn once, I took
because I had to: black, a sort of crêpe
he bought for funerals, and hated.

Reading it again
(*the case is altered*)

The Consul felt a clutch at his heart . . .
If you had sent the postcard
he slips under his wife's lover's pillow,
if you came back, now,
dreaming of the cabin *between the forest*
of pine and high, high, waving alders,
could I reach for you simply, seeing as if with eyes open
again, drinking in your hurt gaze,
or should I reach first
for the bottle of mescal, or bourbon?
Mid-morning heat, a hangover, *eau gazeuse* . . .

*

Our mad captain will attack
the mountain with its quarry at daybreak.
Alone by the swimming pool in total dark
I murmur, *For Christ's sake, for sweet Jesus Christ's sake,*
come back.

A short history of snakes

1

While the pavements throb and sweat
with summer, a steady thumping beat,
you parade and sway and stalk
about the room, a high-heeled, low-hipped walk
from drinks-tray to icebox and back.

From the record-player
come the sounds of swampland or bayou
and also on the air
the reek of dope
curls up like snake-charmer's rope.

Stretched in your armchair,
basking, his tail
in Florida, the forks
of his tongue
in South Carolina, or Texas,

is the Coral Snake –
the one who comes out at night
to bare his single tooth,
his poison fang;
or it might be the Copperhead,

coiled and coloured like a length of wiring,
his noise easily taken for a rattle,
who is 'inoffensive, retiring',
who devours
'whatever is available';

or the Cottonmouth,
the sluggish one, at home
in slow-moving waters, whose bite

'is quite likely to be lethal',
going through his threat-

routine . . . *Don't you ever make such a bad mistake,*
I'd rather fall into bed with a rattlesnake –
the very thing that makes her rich
makes me poor . . . And like a squaw
of the Iroquois, or Sioux,

you will eat,
for cunning, the flesh of the pit-viper, raw.
Don't let that woman make a fool out of you . . .
You can still see the quick nerves twitch,
there is more.

2
It has all gone like a dream,
or so it would seem –

a few drinks, of course,
a few faltering steps on the dance-floor,

his groin pressed tight to yours,
his mouth full of your hair.

A taxi through rain-shining streets.
Then the nightmare

of splintered
glass, a shard

held to your throat
as he puts you through it,

your telephone blaring, off the hook,
a drunken voice on the intercom,

a round spy-hole of light
in the steamed-up window.

The pacing of your neighbour
who is haunted, even now,

by the fact that he mistook
your final, blood-curdling scream

for the noise you often make
when he urges you to come.

*

You wake
in a tangle of sheets,

reach for the familiar, hard
flesh beside your own –

something is there
(though you cannot feel a single bone),

curled around its head,
scaly, rustling, wet.

Without a word,
he slithers out of bed

and down the stone
stairs, stops to light a cigarette.

The introduction

Three men pause a moment in the dazzling air
At the top of the steps.
All three are smiling, as if
For a photograph

You would have taken, had you been there.
One of them stands slightly apart,
At a not quite formal distance.
It is your father.
He introduces the others:
'Mr Forster, this is Mr Cavafy.'
Then, still wearing their awkward smiles,
They go down to the dazzling garden.

It is perfect, the table and the fountains,
The patch of shade
Where two men sit
In white crumpled suits,
At their slight angle to things, which takes in, between sips,
Discreetly, the boy who brings them lemonade.
It is like nearby Eden,
Or a total eclipse
In the middle of the desert.
Your father has gone back inside the house
And watches from his study windows
Something to do with history, or art,

Or something that has nothing to do
With either,
As he now thinks,
His eyes fixed on the skyline of Alexandria.
And what was it
Flaubert said of the Sphinx?
Or was it perhaps the pyramid?
The plump, forbidden fruits
Would sweat it out as Nile slid by,
The flies would dance their seven veils
Above the heads of those two in the cool penumbra,
Mouthing the difficult words, their eyes perfectly happy.

Song

How slender you'd grown,
That last time, after two years
Slipping through my fingers,
More like sand or water
Than the pebble you compared yourself to,
Worn smooth by the kind of sea
That wears you out as well,
And was something to do with me.
I'd already thought you thinner
Than any girl I'd known.

You should be here, my skinny one,
Varnished with oil,
Laid back and burnished by the sun
Or taking a dive –
In every inch as lithe
As a dolphin or an otter;
Turning in the lathe
Of my hands like a length
Of seasoned wood; a subtle coil
Around me, all suppleness and strength.

Except that now the sea's far greener
Than even your eyes' green,
And not so hard to see through.
Its lift and swell
Is like your body sliding under mine,
Its salt pungency
Has the taste of your armpit and groin.
We made a biggish wave –
Your skin the colour of sand,
Your hand squeezing my hand

As it moved on your stomach, your little breasts.
A rush of wet. I was amazed –
You took the wind out of my sails for ever.
Columbus, going west,
Might have fallen off the edge
As I fell out of your bed,
But he fetched up on these islands instead.
To get this far, a river
Has to go its separate ways.
Now it's all water under the bridge.

Imagine my mother dancing

or stopping in the nursery late at night.
She will appear in pearls and a new fur,
a cloud of perfume and a burst of light
from a diamond hair-clip. That's her,
pouring cocktails from a silver shaker
into a glass like an upturned parasol, glancing
at Daddy. Imagine her dancing,
looking over someone's shoulder for a sign
from him – that he's watching her, that he thinks
she's beautiful . . . How her eyes shine,
something to do with all those drinks,
with memory. Stubbing cigarettes in the sand,
pursing her lips for the lipstick/mirror, taking my hand
and drawing me to her suddenly in a crowd
out shopping one afternoon, laughing too loud
at Daddy's jokes. *Imagine my mother dancing.*

Confidence

'Some of them are pearls, my friend would say,
or there are pearls in there somewhere,
for certain, if you can only find them.
And there was something else he said:
You shouldn't ever throw a pearl away.
But I've never been one for that kind of talk.

She was well known around the bars.
She was known, mostly, for that look of hers –
nothing you could really point to –
that put you in your place. It'd flare up,
kind of sudden, and there you'd be,
wondering what you'd said. No guy thinks
that he can take too much of that,
but I can tell you, there were plenty.
Most of them she wouldn't give the time of day.
A hat? Oh sure, she wore a hat.'

Astrology

You wanted to cast my nativity
but it soon came down
to Van Morrison's *Astral Weeks.*
Who but you could read the signs
in a cup of camomile
or rose-hip tea?

I sat in your red-painted kitchen
while you rolled joint after joint
then made up a bed
by piling cushion
on huge scatter-cushion
on the sitting-room floor.

I was about to ask
what was the point
of my sleeping in one place, your
sleeping in another,
but you stood and undressed
and got under the blanket there and then –

you'd help me to divine
the source of my slimed fingers'
curious smell,
learn augury
from a pink fledgling in its nest,
seek out your thigh's small wen

and create a stir
in the firmament; or go
by these, and make them agree –
the single star
in the curtainless window,
the star tattooed on your left breast.

The feather

She would put her heart
into a *tranche d'agneau* or Peking duck,
then while the others were letting themselves go
with a Stilton, say, or a *tarte aux pommes*
she would make her usual excuse,
get out a feather
and tickle herself pink.
At the first swallow
back would come an avocado mousse.
The rest would follow
with all the inevitability of art.

One day, as luck
would have it, the feather slipped down
her throat
as easily as a mouthful of *Beaumes*
de Venise. It cut such a swathe
through the coiled miles of her insides,
those pretty *tripes à la mode de Caen.*
When it came up against her womb
it cut right through it.

She has nothing now to fear
from the mirror with its tell-tale
little-girl-wounded stare,
the lunar tempest
and its capricious tides,
her flesh's lovely, contoured swoop and swell.

*

Before dinner you took down and read
The Unbearable Lightness of Being.

Turning from the sink
I saw my father's lawn
one summer morning
when I was eight,
a little pile of feathers
in the centre, a few artfully scattered
like an early Dubuffet.
Our cat stretched out
on a sunny patch, licking his lips.

We're through with starling *Véronique*
for another week. I peel and portion
a tangerine and spit the pips

and feel the drunkenness I usually feel
when you take the bones from my plate
and crunch them up in your marvellous teeth –
leaving not so much as a splinter.

You smile at me. We climb to bed.
Cat's-eyes. Cat-slink.

PETER McDONALD

The deaf wars

It's nearly over now.
I suppose you've broken cover,
though it makes no odds; the words
shrunk back, unspoken, long ago,
whatever you meant to say.
There's still maybe a year or two

to go before you tell
the whole truth, such as it is.
Tonight a soldier gets loaded
on a tranquilliser cocktail,
gaping at clouds of roses,
the silent blossoms of shells.

Charlie Chaplin went to France
To teach the cannibals how to dance
and here they come,
skipping over the trenches,
each one swinging a time-bomb.
And their theme today is silence.

So the mud has you washed up
on a final high place,
open-mouthed, amazed
in a stalled sign-language
for the last of the comic deaths.
Your smile trickles over the edge.

Killers

You could think of them as hunters,
achieved, professional,
ready for anything.
Their minds are on the job in hand
and their hands are steady.
They've gone by now, most likely,

but in the country, one by one,
the birds are falling
out of the trees, into
another shade of green;
just sparrows, thrushes,
nothing exceptional,

at least nothing you'd notice
in this weather, walking
the wet road home
at closing time, until
there are hands on your arm,
light as feathers.

Out of Ireland

Just how far do you have to go
before you get to the world's edge?
Today, a hard sun lights the snow
for miles, and deep inside his cage

your tame canary sings and dances,
ignoring winter. He has a voice
and uses it, taking no chances.
He entertains, as though he had a choice.

This summer you'll be sailing west,
whether the sea is calm or angry,
until you drop. Your bird knows the rest,
he knows he'll die hungry.

Ideal home

As soon as you open the front door
on to a deep-pile hall carpet
and harvest-gold walls,
you begin the new life.
In the lounge, you sit
smoking, as your wife
fixes some drinks, maybe cocktails.
Already you're asking for more.

It's been like this from the start;
a kitchen that almost runs itself,
the TV, the sleeping video.
In case of emergencies
the basement has enough
food for twenty days,
a purring clock-radio
and an ashtray the shape of a heart.

The third day

for Michael Longley

My head is melting;
smears of hair and flesh-tone
are slipping through the fingers
of hands that are no longer
just so much skin and bone,
and return to where they'd risen

on my grandfather's palette
in some makeshift studio,
a damp back-parlour
in Belfast or Glasgow.
Now, while the paint's wet,
he'll turn the street corner

where my father might wait,
his hair shiny with Brylcreem,
to deliver another telegram
in forties London;
sucking on a boiled sweet,
there's nothing he foresees

that could bring him any closer
to his young son, the grandson,
whose unborn arms and legs
will have grown away from him
like the head that's melting now
with ice cream and Easter eggs.

Consequences

I must be about fourteen or fifteen,
for I seem to be walking through wet
sunlit streets with Andy and Stephen,
and trying to look older than I am,
say seventeen or eighteen, with luck.

Music is pulsing out like morse
to Ann Street and the world
as we flaunt its loud new colours
where later, relishing the danger,
the three of us might share a can of lager.

*

Years ago, in the redbrick school
at Gilnahirk, that spring day
when the master, Mr Peterson,
finally gave Tom Boyd the strap,
the strongest of us winced to see

his hands close on their weals
as he learned his lesson, gradually.
There was something resembling sympathy
in our faces then, but not for long.
Tom Boyd was fat. We hated him.

*

Another one of those long parties
I couldn't get out of. My glass
needs a refill; Dr Stephens
and Mrs Andrewes are addressing themselves
to the question of public sponsorship

for the opera; I must be talking
to a girl who looks nineteen or twenty
about her painting, *The Toy Shop*,
when suddenly our shy host, Mr Morse,
is asking will I step outside one moment.

A prism

How long is it now since the two of us
stood watching the Irish Sea darken
with hardly a word between us?
I can barely recognise myself; your own
face is long gone,
leaving the sea unchanged behind it.

Things go on changing, all the same;
this morning, for instance,
the season loosens, and I walk away
from my seven colours, into
the forgetful light of spring,
as though, somehow, the new life

were really beginning here
and at last I had forgotten
the darkness waiting like a screen
behind and around me
where still, impossibly,
Richard of York gives battle in vain.

Pleasures of the imagination

Again I'm caught staring
at the sky, in particular
those blue-black clouds
that shadow the sun. I remember
I was meant for a painter
and see in a puddle
cause for reflection.

I've packed my bags again
for Cloud-cuckoo land;
you might see me there,
mouth agape, as I recline
on beds of asphodel,
finally reaping the benefits
of a classical education.

But there are other approaches;
the celebrated Donal O'Sheugh
owes his allegiance

to a different culture.
He has carpeted his apartment
in the heart of New Jersey
with the best Irish turf

(perhaps, all the time,
he was speaking in parables).
Not that it matters –
I think I could stay here
amazed by this September
sun-shower, quite silent,
until his cows come home.

Meanwhile, on a deserted
film-set, the handsome
Count Dracula has heard tell
that he is a metaphor now,
and is unhappy.
He aspires to symbolism
and perhaps, one day, to nothing at all.

JO SHAPCOTT

Electroplating the baby

Of the Egyptians the rich alone
were capable of having it done.

The cadavers were immersed
in antiputrescible baths

and then swathed by the relatives
in thousands of bandages.

In our time the art of embalming
has not made much advance:

are our processes so imperfect
as to dull our inclination?

Or do we relish the privacy of dust?
In answer one physician proposes

electro-metallurgy as *the* way
to obtain indestructible mummies.

He metallises our entire cadaver.
He encloses it in an envelope

of bronze, copper, nickel, silver or gold
according to the wealth or caprice

of those who survive.
Does this awaken your curiosity?

Do you wish to know
how Dr Variot proceeds?

In a double frame with four uprights
connected top and bottom by four square plates

is the body of a child which has been
perforated with a metallic rod.

One end of the rod abuts
the arch of the cranium,

the other end is inserted as a pivot
in a metallic bearing at the base of the frame.

The frame support is a conductor of electricity.
The uprights and connecting wires

are carefully insulated
with gutta percha.

The electric current is furnished
by three small 'chaudron' thermo-electric batteries.

A circular toothed metallic contact
descends from the top plate and rests

lightly on the vertex of the cadaver.
The lower surface of the feet

and the palms of the hands
rest upon two contacts.

Before immersing this apparatus
in the electro-metallurgic bath,

it is necessary to render the body
a good conductor of electricity.

To this effect the operator
sprays the skin of the cadaver

with a solution of nitrate of silver
by means of a homely apparatus –

the atomiser used by ladies
for perfuming themselves!

This operation having been performed
the skin becomes of an opaque black

and the silver salt has penetrated
as far as the derma.

Next the silver salt must be reduced;
that is to say, separated from its oxide.

(To do this is very difficult.)
The frame is placed under a glass bell

in which a vacuum has been formed,
and into which vapours of white phosphorus

dissolved in sulphide of carbon
are afterwards allowed to enter.

(This is a dangerous operation
like all operations in which phosphorus

in solution plays any part whatever.)
Then the skin of the cadaver

is of a greyish white.
There is nothing left to do now

but to proceed as rapidly as possible
to the metallisation. To this effect

the frame is immersed in a bath
of sulphate of copper.

(We need not describe this operation
which is known to all.)

Under the influence of the electric current
the deposition of the metal goes on

uninterruptedly. The molecules
of metal deposit on the skin

and soon form thereon a continuous layer.
(The operator must regulate

the passage of electricity with great care
in order to prevent a granular deposit

having but little adhesion.)
By shifting the contacts properly

the operator will substitute for the skin
a coating of copper

which will take on the pattern
of all the subjacent parts.

By attentively watching
the thickness of the deposit

upon the face, hands and all
the delicate parts of the body,

a faithful mould will be obtained
that will exactly recall

the details of conformation
and the tints of the physiognomy.

A deposit of from half
to three quarters of a millimetre

offers sufficient strength
to resist external bendings and blows.

A thickness of from half
to three quarters of a millimetre

ought not to be exceeded
for the metallic covering

of the face and hands
which will be thus perfectly moulded.

Upon the trunk, the abdomen, the neck
and the first segments of the limbs

the integral preservation
of the plastic forms is much less important.

What is the future in store
for this process of mummification?

It would be impossible to say.
It is infinitely probable

that metallised cadavers
will never figure

except in small numbers
for a long, long time to come.

Late snow

A cold spring:
the violet was flawed on the lawn.
Elizabeth Bishop

With cold air advancing from the Arctic
a depression slid over the Irish Sea:
in Cambridge cricketers couldn't grip,
all routes over the Pennines were closed,
power lines tumbled in the Yorkshire Dales.

The sheep liked the snow; it suited their cryptic
coloration. They lived in ice caves like new beasts:
ice breath, ice fleece, rumination and travail –
but their tongues got stuck on the ice
of their own bloody waters frozen round their lambs.

Now, in summer, I listen for cold drinks,
I root in cocktails, hold chilled tea to light –
I'm looking for an ice-cube streaked like a humbug
to hold inside my cheek for the slow melt,
until hooves flutter on my tongue.

Hubei Province tornado

Mrs Yang has experienced
an air adventure. The tornado
that uprooted trees lifted
the umbrella-holding woman
several hundred yards high
into the sky. She crossed
the Jiuda River. She was carried
for five hundred and fifty yards,
then landed slowly. Strangely,
though she was injured by hailstones,
she was intact.

Pete goes swimming

I

You say:
swimming is my forte –

(toesplash across watertop
to demonstrate your domain)

we are like those quarried blocks
over by the bluff

squared off to the lake floor
not floating at all

(you duckdive,
pleased with this thought).

2
Nearby, a flurry
in another group.

They call to you:
we've lost a child.

3
Your foot touches something
cool. *I'll dive if you dive.*

No. You. The child slides away
on an undertow

but the images keep coming:
you'd never touched

someone dead before. Just animals –
and fish (years ago, you'd chased

your sister with a dead trout:
touch it, kiss it).

4
Away over by the bluff
she broke surface: they swung her out

by her heels and passed her
hand to hand through the sun;

a beauty: pearl dead, fish eye –
independent of the air.

With the big tray

Hilary had to mind the tea service
at each end of the long march
up the staircase (those places
by the newel posts where her hips
had to angle and re-angle
at the new levels). Then
there was an impasse
at the bedroom door
where really another person was needed
to get a grip on the ebony handle.
In the event an elbow served
and after wriggling and clinking
round the door like a belly dancer
she found herself inside
foolish on the Moroccan rug.
There had been an audience:
a housefly was swooping by the lilac
in mother's clover vase – the one
Nicholas had thrown for her.
The sun constructed an avenue
to the bedside table
and now the housefly played
boomerang in and out of the light.
Hilary surprised herself by breaking wind,
though secretly her large smell
made her feel as real and salty
as a merchant adventurer.
She would take something for it

from the bathroom cabinet anyway.
She set the tray down by the bed
noting as she did the ornate little table.
It had been made by a local craftsman
and she had, at first, been impressed
by what she interpreted
as the mark of difficulty
that its execution had left on his face.
Now there were more or less
three white rings on the walnut veneer.

DOMINIC FISHER

Elvers

Trimmed fish flatter than snakes
and more sophisticated than worms.
Each is a self-sufficient muscle
packed in an elastic sheath.

From gill to gill the wide-eyed heads
split open to a fringed maw.
Toothed baby faces wailing in silence,
gaping and closing, gaping and closing.

Inert in their artificial river bed
exposing lengths of cable.
Coming live and making
currents through the gravel.

Flexible missiles in a tank
that trail off to fishy ribbon.
Year-old elvers responding
to impulse in a closed circuit.

Gothic script

Gothic script on thick paper
– a curious deed
in dead-letter copperplate.

These horror-film characters,
all hooks and folded wings,
are not really letters;

they are more a paragraph
of funeral emblems, ur-swastikas
and japanned fleurs-de-lis.

Indecipherable runes
in glossy columns with footnotes
in Latin and English.

Between black ideogram and
something found under a stone,
each is the word for itself.

Evenly spaced in families –
representatives of the order
Coleoptera. A collection of beetles,

a testimony to the collector's
dedication to order and variety,
in manuscript under a glass.

Something about a wood,
a dead rook, ritualised contests
on invisible highways.

An adequate translation
will always elude us
despite the once wriggling words
having been pinned to the paper.

An exhibition of samplers

Pecking back into the fabric,
burrowing to the surface,
making soft ice – a needle
in small hot fingers.

Seams of hand-made limestone
with veins of spider-work,
with even the finest membrane
of fossil plants preserved.

Cipher stars in dense conjunctions
with no interpretation
beyond the biblical intended.

'Our Father Which Art in Heaven
Hallowed be Thy Name.'

The house of virtue homely
in the centre of the field
that is complexedly bordered
and has no horizon.

Vases descended from Italy
and erstwhile griffons
in the linen gardens with topiary
where bands of animals sometimes
process and repeat like nursery tales.

A bright point worming in ennui
to make crystals in a bleached ground
in the early eighteenth century.

*

'My Mother.
Who fed me from her gentle breast
And hushed me in her arms to rest
And on my cheek sweet kisses pressed,
My mother.'

It was not originality that was prized
but the work and the diligence
with which it was done.

Representation waxed and waned
donating motifs of God's house and creatures,
depicting home with its windows and its hedge.
Hands must not be idle.

Small girls took the elements of their work –
the strips and shapes of model vegetable patches
or trays of tiny cakes, the urns and candelabra trees
that could be fountains – from cloth diaries.

'She seeketh wool and flax and worketh
Willingly with her hands.'

*

Mary Jeffries' rubric-red exemplar is
file on file of alphabets and numerals like Letraset,
the whole of which is bounded with such border work
as three years hence would be required of her.
In the centre is a lozenge labelled 'Bible'
and below that is her name and the year 1867.
Continuing down, as though on an envelope
well-addressed to herself is the legend:
'North Wing,
New Orphan House,
Ashley Down,
Bristol.'

Her parents were cholera victims so, child of the dead,
from the age of five she was raised in charity to go
at eighteen into service as a nursemaid in Birkenhead.

*

'Brethren the time is short.'

*

When scarcely more than infant, Annette Arabella Mitchell
formed her first letters in cross-stitch,
learning not to prick her fingers and stain the work
or fall asleep for a hundred years.
In 1886, poised demurely on the bench
drawing coloured thread through cloth
for a seeming eternity and entrusted, perhaps,
with the instruction of little ones, she was
stitching her way towards womanhood
– girl on the cusp working a view
of the parish church as a vignette
below the name of her school.
And in that tranquil world of hand-worked underclothes,
of seams, pleats, ruffles and tucks and pins
of that last year, the dark blood moved.

*

'Prize the one thing needful.'

*

The small children of extinct social classes
strained their sight and gave exquisite patience
in the practice of extinct accomplishments.
The children of new social classes,
shown the work in an exhibition of samplers,
ask, 'Could you do that when you were seven, Mum?'
The disclaimer comes low-voiced and quickly,
like modesty.

On the walls there are futures,
faded but conserved, as defined and set
as a border, as pre-ordained
as the sequence of the alphabet.

The Bristol box-kite

Parcels of space for the wind
hung like an art work
from the ceiling's flat fog.

A plan in wire, wood and paper
that is the thing itself
for a voyage into the future.

The open frame of laminated
bentwood would seat a rowing blue,
some all-rounder, a university man
game for a spot of derring-do.

Beneath the snarl of the engine sculling
the blades of the screw at the pilot's rear
there would be a rhythm of creakings as though
a leather seat was being flown through the air.

From the museum ceiling
we could climb on a purring coil
up to the ultramarine

and look back down at the little world
changing with our leaving of it and enthralled
for ever now by things from the sky.

One sick harp-string note of springing wire
and we might fold up in the air or dive down
as hard as a kite with its tail gone.

'Look, see the aeroplane?'
'Where, where?' 'There; look, there!'
The child at the gallery balustrade
sees no shark-shaped jet,
only suspended abstract boxes with sticks.

'There's its wings, there's its tail.'
Foxed, the child still does not see a plane.
Could this be adult make-believe again?

Back to front

The telephone sleeps in the shape of a cat
outside the window. The wind plays

desultory xylophone with a child's
rising and falling enthusiasm.

Dangling paint-spattered wires dream messages
of rapid morse in a core of twisted copper.

Leaves massed, each holding a portion of thick sky,
make the sound of a radio tuned between stations.

A carpenter saws a length of afternoon; its end drops
to the damp coconut of sawdust on the flagstones.

A man called in to patch patching-up up
whistles as he heals the weeping wall. Nearby –
a hammering as of a clock the size of a wardrobe.

On the road a part of last night's paper
gabbles drunkenly to itself.
At the front the traffic passes at full volume.

Details of kitchens are half exposed, cisterns flush.
At the front at street doors people adjust their dress,
step smartly, and vehicles print colour on the tarmac.

At the front it is Friday night tomorrow already.
Out the back the minutes and hours of Thursday afternoon
are still being haphazardly fitted together.

Genesis

One of those days when things
always seem to take an age.
But, inevitably, there was change
on removing major items from the landscape.

Creatures that had had a niche in the debris
migrated, adapted, died out.
Mountains gave way to coal forest.
The stegosaurus went with the paper.

Ichthyosaurs and plesiosaurs disappeared
as the plug was pulled out of the sink.
Meanwhile, cadres of small furry beasts
were awaiting the dinosaurs' downfall.

During the washing up the mammals got larger,
grew sabre-toothed, and ruled in their turn.
Then there was climatic turmoil when
the kitchen window was opened.

Later, trekking across Africa, where a late
Pleistocene breakfast had been – the first hominids.
It had taken half a billion years
just to clear the kitchen table.

PIPPA LITTLE

Witch burning country

In East Anglia a tree marks the focus
of no particular place. They say this one

was a witch's grave. Mushrooms do circle it,
knuckling up out of the blue, dead grass.

The wind has a smell to it here, of
old blood rotting in the sap. The tree's

a needle, through which the sun
has burned all night. I closed

and opened my eyes to it, to mornings
as a child, waking out of death.

My bones shiver in this heat,
wanting to walk home four hundred years.

Sky's long white skeins drift out,
fens blow with ashes, the black road's melting.

Minotaur

Wrecked church,
unravelled winding-sheet:
the silence is a rock, it can't
be rolled back
to release this dark
incense of bones –

who was he shut his faith in here, in hope
of resurrection?

Unblessed, dead place,
still you ache for miracles – hating
the old stories like dreams from a fever,
yet wanting Lazarus
here,
as if
you were the one his white face turned to first.

Mistress of two kitchens

You came to see me with your lake-water eyes
and on my staircase I was mistress of two kitchens
aware of my skeleton sensed between your palms.

My existence I owned: had paid for it already
still you came to give me others, an orchestra –
I could be streetlights turning blue

or the fizzle of rain across a river;
instead I offered coffee, attempting to recall
without shivering, to control my slippery surface

enough to send you skimming into my chair-arms.
Look, you said, at the twin trees: you meant one
small, leafy, in a window pot, the other windy, rangy

on the worldly side of the glass. The bang
of a car in the street caught my heart
and you were the same, too perfect, too precise

to face without caution – the arrogance golden
on you like pollen and the beautiful childlike mind
weaving parasols for my trapeze.

Set, in a triangle on my cushion, your ankle
on the other knee in some learned male stance,
questioning my two kitchens. For you my guilt

lied that each was spotless, motherly-clean.
In fact they were privately slack
as half-practised music. Your waterfall words

tangled in my hair, and swept all emotional
arrangements of roses out, for philosophies
brought in secret from basement bars and high

political apartments, the dark French cinemas,
from wherever you came to see me: look, you said,
in delight to find something real in my small tree

when it shook in sympathy with the stronger other;
so I said again – sensing
it was the thing you came to me to hear –

that it seemed to me we were those twins.
But I saw them as a mechanism
plotted to steer a course of slow ruin

across the self-effacing glass, knowing
myself, the mistress of two kitchens,
as that anorexic surface

chafed by two saw-toothed egos:
yours not less beloved
for being the gentler.

Colonial returning

In this house the past is tidal, a wave
always on the point of breaking.
Doorframes shiver in the slightest wind.
Clocks continue, now: now: now:
only they keep the wave solid.
It is an act of will. In dreams,
increasingly, everything is swept away,
bloodily uprooted.

Careful as a visitor
you spread cracks all the same,
you sense vibration,
hear water massing like bees,

a trigger, returning to the storehouse,
treasure-chest, depleting it year by year.
A gentle, loving weakening –
the walls rub thinner, the water's wearing in.

Outside, your homeland's fragile also. Walk
where the sea eats the dunes, little by little
high and low tide. On the horizon
something too heavy to be supported
gathers power to rise.

Fear of heights

Big-shouldered, boxy as chocolate
you craned me
up, up, up
to squat forked behind your neck,
seasick with your every footstep –
the world you made for me too huge.

Later, teaching me to ride, catapulting
me from safety into speed when you let go:
my state of balance molten, I swam
dizzy and grateful down between the handlebars
into the dust; the world you made for me
too sudden, too fast.

Father, I still go reeling in your heights,
hurtling downwards as your hands pull loose:
waking always just upon impact
in the world you made for me.

Sea coal

Thin square-shouldered men
scrape in the sea's wash
for coal,
hauling it out shining, seeming
still spongy: the beach runs blue
indigo.

Men long unemployed
and striking miners
fill bucket after bucket at the shallows,
arms and legs awash, glistening up to the joints;
trudge up the beach to the cart and the bored mare
grinding seagrass down between pale gums.

An east wind slashes in,
one man shivers, his bony shoulderblades
contract. The muscles work blue in his arms,
his shoes are crusted with sand and salt.

For one cold mile along the shore
ragged with dirty dunes, as far

as the power station breezing its cloud
of brilliant detergent,
the sea coal rises with the tide
far out, converges and comes in.

Dead wasp

Crisp in its cocoon –

who wrapped you so neat and tight,
weightless parcel,
                    and then the bleaching rage
drove me to hunt you out, not knowing
you were there:

– will I be dead as you?

I've turned my feather bed,
made best of something going bad,
each knuckle's red from scrubbing,

still I know you. Curled up,
tucked in like a child, but I could blow you
clean away: giant again,
stamping my bloody boots.

I've stripped down to the bricks
motherly as this poor, scraped house
still licked from the operation.

Here we are –
                    you past caring,
rustling as I touch you like the layers
of my mother's old, stiff gowns.
They whispered too.

– You'll go on from here
out of my adult house.

All one to you, anyway.
You did what you came to do.

A year: September

Out on the road
torsos of light
twist malleable as wet steel
off a production line,
make hissing weather.

Passing the hospice
your year-old self accelerates.
Again and again
the moment is made,
takes fire,
is gone.

Here you lie, your arm crescent
for a head forming desires
nameless as bullets.

At such heights, some
details are lost.
And looking back
those snaking nerves of light
seem carved as horn.

LACHLAN MACKINNON

Handcarts

I put my foot down and discovered a city,
an ant pushing an egg like a refugee's handcart,
another, a serious pram-race, touching
antennae to taste one another's terror.

The little shops have been broken open and spill
souvenirs and newspapers on the pavement.
Such redemptive, peripheral sadness while the black
militia point our feet toward the outskirts.

'We walked between columns of smoke. Nobody dreamed
of the immaculate, brick-by-brick restoration
of the Old Quarter, the university,
the medieval ghetto, the Catholic shrine.'

They were back within minutes, working like Trojans
or Germans, jobbing builders, entrepreneurs
and their parasites, ragpickers and dudes with knives . . .
by-blows of the queen ant's lethal forgetfulness.

October

We have lived in small towns hard by the sea.
Even the lorries
seemed to have come to take the waters,
stiff-spined
in the difficult streets.

The woods thrashed like tethered water,
the municipal paddling-pool
spilled in the browned, nervous hands

of our estuary coast.
Stale ocean backed up into fresh,

the dry, miniature gullies filled and pulsed
like a frog's web under a microscope.
The world was glistening with wet.
When the old men speak of your promise,
remember that it is not made to them.

Dial F for fun

Dinner in these motels is almost warmer
than the memory of a bachelor flat. They've even
washed the fingerprints off his telephone. After the wine
he feels as distant as America, lust
blazing like taillights on the thruway:

'What's your bag, baby?' they would say in L.A.,
but here it's 'Which service do you require?'
Offered the catalogue, he asks for Sukie,
Sukie whose thing is lace and innocence surprised,
the sheathed claws of a raunchy debutante.

In L.A. she would be a prom queen, want
The Eagles on the eight-track cartridge player,
but here her opening whispers are as shy
as the daughter's who opens your host's door
in her new blue dress with its velvet collar

until, until the ash loneliness of the small hours
pins him with insomnia to his mattress,
his cigarette-end a will o' the wisp
between his lips and darkness
– rear lights
of a car lit up like a Jack o' Lantern . . .

Baby bunting

The tall policeman
smiles from his taller horse.
'So your mother's alone?
I'll be around.' The coarse

not-in-front-of-the-children chuckle
of his chum on the pavement
only adds to the pickle
I never meant.

I never speak to strangers.
How should I know
my voice is louder than I think?

My friend won't go.
He is ogling the horse's harness,
the truncheon on its flank.

Hopkins in Wales

A sheep nibbling earth's firstlings is my spirit
that prays for the day Christ may stoop me
as a cooper denies his timber's nature –
for two years in this windy eye of God
I have wrestled and prayed against myself
and you ask if I have the time for poems . . .
Your letter brought me tears, and I was grateful.
Oppression, expression, these are words
but lack the radish-bite of right words
for two years in the flinty field
of etymology. *Aneurin*, for example,
is *honour*, maybe, passed down from the Romans
and fading like the faces on their coins –

or is 'little-all-gold', an honorific
for a tanned baby. So Aneurin ap Caw
was the little-all-gold-one of the flowing muse;
words are riddles I dare not answer,
to crack them cracks my heart. Men come to us
and tell God what they cannot tell their wives
and sometimes things press forward at me
begging to speak, symbols, hallucinations –
if I fix my mind with a bare tree,
a frozen spray of being, why always
does it remind me of the bare fork'dness
I must become and cannot? Pray for me and mine,
my brothers in this desolation;
I will not write again, for I am no-one,
and must be nothing but the wind's creak
that flays this earth's responding stubbornness.

Monterey cypress

The tall sad house
blew open every spring
– gusts from the street,
a dusty hall

where the telephone was
that never rang
with invitations
I waited in for.

The tall sad tree
behind the house
was dying, brown
in patches

where the fungus had bitten,
shabby
as a camouflaged helmet
on a parade-ground

and lonely,
stranger than us,
a foreigner
from California.

A lightning-conductor
we both felt,
and surely one
for sorrow.

Here

The disappearance of time, a life as orderly
as the formal view with its row of poplars
and the sleeping river, which at the mill
was brilliance but now has found its level
lower, less limber; these and these alone

are offered by this city with no echoes
where leaves by the cathedral murmur
obliquely their little snide exclusions
and the tobacconists remember the dead.
A woman here would be housed among women,

making love and a tray of muffins
with the same tranquillised complacency –
or say wildly, *When I was sent for mending*
I was limp and unbuttoned, torn by carelessness:
now, light shines through the pinpricks in my arms.

This is a man's world of leather bindings
and football posts bowed down by swinging children.
A file of boys appears in the early mist,
shuffling to showers, muddied, jogging half-crouched
as though they feared the mist would turn to gas.

Crystals

You remember chemical transformations
vaguely, in the prehistory before exams
counted for much. They were done in the wooden lab that
 smelt
of dangerous acids, comical ether
– somebody passed out, having soaked his handkerchief.
The best was copper sulphate, gathering
its crystal round the necessary thread.
Are crystals held together by flaws?
Chemical transformations! and the result of one is
you wake up in tears and can do nothing all day.

Low water

The sea toys with its food, pushes it
to the side of its plate, planks, oilcans,
dead handkerchiefs. The sea has grown up
into some terrible kind of slob.
It watches too much television.
It slurps the froth off its drink without looking.
Its analyst recommends a change
but it has no plans to go anywhere,
do anything. It lolls. Gulls pick at the leavings
in its lap as it drowses past lighting-up time.

Its vast lethargy crumbles stones and shells.
We hardly dare speak of survival
though survival is what it has achieved.
We hold hands, the first time in weeks;
what I should wear to my doctor
was the last dilemma I teased you with,
a torchbeam in the fog around my thoughts.
This great torpor is the prelude to cure.
We may yet hear the sound we came for,
the sea stirring, rattling its bars of shingle.

ADAM THORPE

Marmoreal

for my mother

It's *circa* nineteen fifty-seven, all the lawns
afflicted with a static of leaves, the streets
still cobbled and angling the Art Deco Citroëns
parked there. The Metro's trains have manual doors;
our windows swing with a shunt of metal

tongue that rocks the glass . . . through the net
the casements need re-painting. Look, the scent
of a courtyard curled with cats, steps
entranced by their stone banisters flanked by
bollards we'll flake climbing on: the worn

balls of the *belle époque*! Open
the courtyard doors; our flat wafts with winds
off the Seine, Madame Boppe bustling in
with flowers for the hell of it. Every morning
you trundle my pram along the Quai d'Orsay

all the way to the Musée Rodin, its gardens
littered with bits of Carrara, marmoreal.
Look, I am getting used to my appendages
of fists amid blanket and monument; rock
in the wordless despair of incontinence. These smooth

Olympuses of chin pass, unabashed
by dribble, the emergent struggle from snot and the tang
of saliva from your handkerchief: Think
or Kiss undisturbed by the leaves' crackle.
Effloresced on the surface of my vision

they begin to harden, more dependable
than flesh. One turns slowly as we bump
towards it: torso wracked, each bled eyeball
blank and wide round its drilled retina:
the gaze of the immortal! You start to hum

some Georges Brassens to swathe the clamour of me
and the bronze agony of the Burghers of Calais,
ridiculed by pigeon-shit. The borders of my vision
shift uncontrollably: our maternal diptych
already, for example, near the murmur of the Quai

approaching the empire of the vast Pont
d'Alexandre-Trois, its streaked viridian of lamp
and cherub towering over us. Each subject it carries
I exact a smile from: while something silvery
moves ceaselessly beneath them, ignoring me.

Nature studies

Raring to go, amused
by summer, the chrysalis
broke open, flew from the jam-jar

an ivory petal.
The emptied vessel
stank of grass, of someone's breath

too long withheld.
The cress, too, grew fat
and lazy, from stubble to beard

on the coal-bunker.
From Woolworth seed
these dahlias have risen

bigger than fists, red
and swollen. An orange tree
in a pot by the sink

winks tiny fruit, three
sucked hearts of gobstoppers
on spindly leaves.

I'm graduating to terrapins,
the next order, with brains
and an inkling of love.

The shells must not go soft,
they like bananas.
Summer will see them

bask on the crazy-paving
in a riot of creation
all made by me, aged ten-and-a-quarter.

Grass, trees, butterflies,
a litter
of emptied jam-jars.

Rabbits are easy, as long
as you watch the foxes – and then,
in a special tank, I'd like

to grow a whale, creaming
the heated water so that
the neighbours would notice

its glittering spume arc high
in the Buckinghamshire sky.
What next? Well, looking in the mirror

I reckon
I could have a go at that,
when I'm older.

Childhood visit

Pre-war Dinkies of a frail zinc
glassed from thumbs; my dread of the breathless, domed
bell the moon embalms – of its flowers looming
        skeletal arms,

dead as Grandpa. Bedded in drifts of sheets he
might have kneed, drowned in the stench of naphtha-
lene, I fold my hands as the clock begins to
        clear its sarcophagus,

gong its hour in long, seismotic moans of
cogs, unclouding midnight. The curtains, belled by
moon, sigh their hems on its phosphorescence,
        flap up to blind

clock, chair, table, bedknob; the twin reflected
eyes I fail to recognise. Cobwebbed corners
yield to sight: are drained of their mysteries;
        caught in the glare their

spiders curl like kindled magnesium, flared from
silence. Winds unpin me from shadow, slide me
loomed across the ceiling and down the wall to
        bump on the floor with

swollen profile, hair in a dazzle, hand un-
folded from its prayer. Then darkness, sudden,
tents the room. The curtains, absolved from light,
        swoon to their sills; the

clock taps patient, waiting for dawn: I'm shawled in
sleep . . . Matlock voicing its blackened stone from
moor to moor as rainfall begins to lisp its
        useless instructions.

Camargue

In the tall, cold, Victorian classroom
with its windows fixed so no-one could see
anything interesting to distract them,

hunched beside the empty desk still innocently
sloped for Timothy – who'd slid off Snowdon
banging his pick-axe in the handle-end

and bumped six hundred feet too far
from us and this classroom – I'd stare at the one
tacked image of freedom – three white horses

planing the endless shallows of the sunned
Camargue. The photographer was somehow above them –
flying, no doubt. The water had hidden the land,

so it seemed as if the horses galloped on the weight
of ocean, foamed where each of their hooves hit it.
Wind in their manes, and the eight letters of the name

a simple kind of spell on the peeled wall:
CAMARGUE. We finally went there, last year,
and the sun had dried the marshes up so mud

popped and burbled, or cracked its flats. A couple
from Paris got their Citroën stuck, she
immaculately hopping like a stork

in her white dress; he peeled to his underpants
slipping and floundering around the wheel like a Sumi
wrestler, black to his neck, shovelling bark

under the rutted tyre, grunting with anger.
A passing warden of the *Parc National*
shrugged one shoulder, a prophetic deity

weary of the struggles of humanity. Five
thousand francs, he pouted, if they happened
to be caught by a *Parc* policeman. He tossed his head –

et vous aussi, pour les aider! The heat
shimmered on the Vaccarès. We slapped at gnats
as the woman hopped, attempting take-off in a blur

of hands, her lipstick blooming begonia-red.
Eventually a Range-Rover towed them out,
a great gouge spun from the smooth marsh-bed.

And all the horses we saw were ridden, tin-cans
littering the hoof-marked flats, drained of disguise.
Each night we were bitten, swarms rising from the gorse

of the camp-site. We finally walked the beach from Stes-
Maries-de-la-Mer, striding through sand with the wind
on our nakedness, the world suddenly unafraid

of its first frailties, glorying in skin. We smacked
through foam; entered yelling the warmth of ocean
the soaring universe bumps its rump on.

Egg packing station, Wiltshire

It's difficult to find anything
interesting to say about it:
I read Lawrence's *Apocalypse*
between the boxes, those short breaks

which on Waitrose days were few,
if ever; his attack on St Francis
hovering unread in the middle
of its sentence as the lids

slid into the cardboard exterior
and the tape twisted to seal it
from the tape-cutter. Sometimes
the lids ran out, or the labels

gummed together, or the tape
refused to cut at the flick of the wrist
(an acquired skill) and yards of it
would web as the belt crammed with boxes.

It got me excited, *Apocalypse*:
sweeps of history obliterated
almost completely the chatter
of the perpetual radio, its speaker

vying manfully with the regular
bass of the sorter and the belt's rumble,
the shrieks and laughter of the personnel
typing letters on the heads of eggs

as they coffined them in sixes, each bubbling
down the sorter to oblivion. Until
the supervisor tapped my shoulder
as supervisors have done for millennia

and informed me that reading was forbidden.
Apocalypse-less, I grew depressed
at the expectation of an eternity
of eggs; even the buzzer failed

to cheer me: crouched over tea
in the fogged canteen, the news of the village
excluded as code does. I read
the backs of crisp-packets, learning

about the longest car in the world
or the record for log-rolling, who
survived the highest fall, landing
in deep snow without a parachute.

There was Mike, sixteen, not
considering anything but this
'because the Bomb'll drop'. Sue
who I stumbled into as she was kissing

Ellen, ginger and androgynous,
in the doorway after the shift
with frost already thick on the road.
I liked all of them: and after

walking alone on the chalk downland
their voices were warm, and their laughter
something unassailable. Each night
at the end, tired and aching,

we mopped up the broken ones
that failed to make it: yolks and albumen
swirled into buckets, like some
terrible abortion, apocalyptical.

We were, of course, tender with our own:
each cradled a dozen (we had them cheaper)
in a queue to clock our cards at nine
in the machine, and out into

air like a thirst of iced water
drinking us up: walking past
the management consultant's thatched
cottage with its Lautrec poster

and pinewood furniture we stopped
to wrap our coats closer: snow
all over the downs to Marlborough,
the blackthorn exact in the swing of headlamps.

On leave

Well – we heard a rumble and a cough before us
and a hauling-in of cloaks, rich it was
but dim-hushed, and on approach we stenched
a sweetness:

hemp-seed burnt in a cauldron-censer
(bronze, birch-hugged handles) – sends
y'mind and blows y'chin-strap does it half!
We took 'em

then without a whimper. Well – y'know
the soggy grain we found near Camulodunum
with all the dead-'uns deep in the clunch-pit,
the clasp

you pocketed, the gold molar? It were
the rising of the brain, like when Poenius-boy
boiled it rotten and Cerilius tossed up his guts
on the shield-

leather. Like enough to stuff the Ninth
down Paradise-way and screw off the cold
with the twenty crater of mulsum nicked
from harbour.

Like as not you'd suck y'pizzle to get
a whiff of this: not a cowshit-stopped reed-shaft
but a vestal ticklin' y'baubles near the Agrippa –
or the crunch

and the crushed femur
in the lady-killer's ludi
when the rag-tag bursts
around ye!

O friend, I grant
'ye are na blate', but remember the time
we walked the seven hills, and the curlew split
with a sling-shot; you left a string of violets

for Mother,
clambered up the Palatine
where the she-wolf milk was sucked and laughed
like the blood-smeared boys at Lupercalia

dangling
their goat-skin strips, and told me how I should die;
like the haruspices and their fondled livers
littering the slab you peered and saw instead

yourself
curled in the curlew-gut, and blubbered,
and ran to the temple to pray with upturned palms
and incense? Remember, friend, *quod cinis es* –

and sometime unto ashes you must return.

To my father

One of the ways we communicate
is the Bugatti meeting at Prescott:
father and son wreathed in Castor
and Methanol, somewhat poor relations
between the billowing tents – you selling yours

in '63, unable to pay for its 'restoration'
after years of topping ninety down the Quai d'Orsay.
I stand uncertain in the blue tear-drops
lined for the Concours, the judges
dissembling their preferences in arcane conversation,

you fingering the polished dashboard
of a Type 37, the one day of the year
a private vocabulary is shared – drop head coupé,
wet multiple plate clutch as a type of transmission,
crankshaft, flywheel, cambox, and the stamp of Molsheim.

Our faces distorted, pulled in the curve
of waxed body-shell the heavens are envious of,
we lean together in a scent of upholstery
the sunlight flexes, its hot leather
breathing a memory of chivalry in the Targa Florio

of '29, Silverstone and Brooklands
and the Mont Ventoux hill-climb.
Pennants flutter above the lunch-tent
as the marshals gather; after our picnic
of Brie and Rivaner, we prop our elbows on the fence

and watch the members 'having a go'
up the hill, puffing the sand at the corners,
double de-clutching in a roar

of eight cylinders and rubber. Nothing matters
but how one takes the horseshoe bend and the sudden

ascent. We race each other in the Renault,
you yelling as I spin slightly
to ease perfectly from first to fourth;
both in a blur of trees and people
disputing our respective times, then glad they were equal.

BIOGRAPHICAL NOTES

ALAN JENKINS was born in 1955, in London. Educated there and at the University of Sussex, he has worked since 1980 for *The Times Literary Supplement*, where he is Fiction and Poetry Editor. Reviews and poems have appeared in *The Times Literary Supplement*, *New Statesman*, the *Observer*, *Encounter* and *Poetry Review*. He won an Eric Gregory award in 1981. He lives in London.

PETER McDONALD was born in Belfast in 1962. He was educated at Methodist College, Belfast and University College, Oxford, where he gained a first in English Literature. Some of his early poems appeared in *Trio Poetry 3* (Blackstaff Press, 1982), and he was awarded the Newdigate Prize in 1983. He was co-editor of *Oxford Poetry* from 1983–5 and his verse-play *Light* was produced in Edinburgh in 1984 and at the Soho Poly, London, in 1985. At present, he researches and teaches in Oxford where he is completing a critical study of Louis MacNeice. His poems and reviews have appeared in *The Honest Ulsterman*, *Poetry Review*, *Fortnight*, *Gown*, *Oxford Poetry*, *Verse* and *North*.

JO SHAPCOTT's poems have appeared in various magazines and anthologies including *South West Review* and *New Poetry 9*. In 1982 she received a South West Arts literature award and in 1985 she won the National Poetry Competition, having been a runner-up in 1983. She has recently moved from Devon to London, where she works as an arts administrator.

DOMINIC FISHER was born in 1953 in Frome, Somerset, the son of an architect and the eldest of nine children, and he grew up in Bath. After secondary education at St. Brendan's College in Bristol, he obtained a Joint Honours degree in Art and English at the University College of Wales, Aberystwyth, where he also trained as a teacher. He did various odd jobs in the Aberystwyth area before becoming a teacher of English as a Foreign Language. He has taught in Turkey and also in Spain (where he met his wife, a New Zealander). Since returning to Britain in 1982 he has concentrated on teaching and writing. He won second prize in the York Penguin Bookshop Poetry Competition in 1984 and is joint author with his wife of the EFL publication *Discover Britain* (Cambridge University Press, 1985).

PIPPA LITTLE was born in East Africa of Scottish parents, but lived in Scotland for most of her childhood. She has been writing since she was a child and won a *Daily Mirror* poetry prize in their children's poetry competition when she was eleven. She has had several jobs, including editorial work on women's magazines and in children's publishing, and has also worked as a cleaner while writing a novel (unpublished). She is now a research student, working on self-images in modern poetry. Her poetry and short stories have been widely published in magazines and anthologies in Britain, America, Canada and India. In 1980 she was one of the winners of a Young Poets Competition in Glasgow, judged by Edwin Morgan. In 1983 *Edges*, a small collection of poems, was published by Ampersand Press. In 1985 she received an Eric Gregory award. She has worked on translations of Hungarian poetry